Olympiad ACE

A Comprehensive Practice Book
for School Olympiads & Talent Search Exams

COMPUTER
Class 2

by
Debapriya Chakraborty

Bloom Cap Edu Ventures Pvt. Ltd.

卐 **Administrative & Production Office**

'Ramchhaya' 4577/15, Agarwal Road, Darya Ganj, New Delhi -110002
Tele: 011- 47630600, 43518550

卐 **PRICE:** ₹125.00

卐 **PO No :** TXT-XX-XXXXXXX-X-XX

Published by Arihant Publications (I) Ltd.

For further information about the books log on to
www.bloomcap.org

Follow us on   

"Future belongs to those Who prepares for it today"

School Olympiads are National & International level competitions conducted by different Government, Non-Government & Educational Organisations with the purpose of making the children ready to face competitive exams.

The challenging Questions asked in Olympiads motivate them to learn more & more and bring out the best result with improved academic performance. The Awards & Scholarship offered by Olympiads motivate children to aspire & strive for doing better and emerge out to be the best.

Science Olympiads

Being a Scientist or Engineer or Doctor has always been a dream of each school going child. A good command over Science is a must for any of these. Questions of Science Olympiads are structured to help students to develop scientific temperament & motivate them to understand the concepts of science. They also focuses on improving existing knowledge of a student by adding more information.

'Bloom Science Olympiad Study Book Class 2' is a perfect resource to Study & Practice for Olympiad Exams and other National & State Level Talent Search Exams & Other Competitions.

Some Special Features of Bloom Science Olympiad Study Books are;

- Chapterwise Exercises having different types of Objective Questions; Analytical, Applications, Remembering etc, at par with the Olympiad Level.
- Detailed Explanation for each question.
- Olympiad Pattern Practice Sets at the end.

This book is prepared by Expert Panel with the utmost care, still if you have any suggestions regarding its improvement then feel free to contact us at support@bloomcap.org. We will try to inculcate your suggestions in the further editions.

Contents

01

Introduction to Computer

1. Computers have .... generations.
   - (a) Six
   - (b) Seven
   - (c) Five
   - (d) Four

2. UNIVAC and ENIAC are examples of .... generation of computers.
   - (a) First
   - (b) Second
   - (c) Third
   - (d) Fifth

3. Which of the following is not a characteristics of computer?
   - (a) An electronic machine
   - (b) Forgets easily
   - (c) Accurate
   - (d) Works faster

4. Second generation of computers used
   - (a) vacuum tube
   - (b) transistor
   - (c) motors
   - (d) ICs

5. .... can operate on batteries and hence are very popular with travellers.
   - (a) Mainframes
   - (b) Laptops
   - (c) Microprocessors
   - (d) Hybrid

6. Which among the following is a feature of computer?
   - (a) Slow working
   - (b) Multitasking
   - (c) Emotional
   - (d) Not intelligent

7. ………… is known as the Father of Modern Computers.
   - (a) Blaise Pascal
   - (b) Henry Fayol
   - (c) Charles Babbage
   - (d) Bill Gates

8. Which of the following keeps the computer ON for a few minutes if electricity goes OFF?
   - (a)
   - (b)
   - (c)
   - (d)

9. Which of the following best describes a Desktop?
   - (a) It is computer data.
   - (b) It is an electronic machine.
   - (c) It is screen that you can see after logging in on windows.
   - (d) It is computer Information.

10. Which generation of computer uses Artificial Intelligence?
    - (a) Third
    - (b) Fifth
    - (c) Sixth
    - (d) Second

11. The orders that you give to a computer are called
    - (a) processing
    - (b) inputs
    - (c) outputs
    - (d) instructions

12. Which of the following statements is/are correct regarding the given device?
    - (a) It is a machine which runs on electricity.
    - (b) It can store information for longer period of time.
    - (c) It does not get tired and can work for hours.
    - (d) All of the above

13. Computer always works on the principle of

(a) yes or no   (b) right or wrong

(c) input and output   (d) hardware and software

14. Computer can perform the same operations with the same accuracy again and again without getting

(a) lazy   (b) serious

(c) funny   (d) tired

15. Which computer type would a pharmaceutical company use to test drugs?

(a) Supercomputer   (b) Mainframe

(c) Laptop   (d) PDA

16. ………. is used to record voice, music and sound into the computer.

(a)   (b)

(c)   (d)

17. Which type of computer is excellent for storing diary dates and addresses?

(a) Laptop   (b) Personal Digital Assistant (PDA)

(c) Desktop PC   (d) Mainframe

18. Which type of computer would a businessman would likely use on a train?

(a) Supercomputer   (b) Mainframe

(c) Desktop PC   (d) Laptop

19. Which type of computer would most likely be used by students in an ICT room?

(a) Laptop   (b) PDA

(c) Desktop PC   (d) Mainframe

20. A device that allows the user to see the information generated by computer is called an

(a) input device   (b) storage device

(c) output device   (d) None of these

21. Where do we get data after processing?

(a) Mouse   (b) Keyboard

(c) Monitor   (d) CPU

22. Which of the following devices does not have touchscreen feature?

(a)    (b) 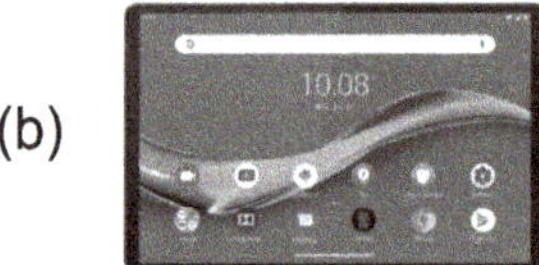

(c)    (d) All of these

23. Which of the following is incorrect about first generation of computers?

(a) The computers were very fast in calculation.

(b) The computers were large in size.

(c) In those days, these were the only electronic devices.

(d) These computers could store information for longer period of time.

24. Both computer and calculator can do calculation. There is one thing that computer can do but calculator can't do. Which one of the following can be done by computer and not by calculator?

(a) Addition   (b) Division

(c) Comparison   (d) Multiplication

25. Given below are the statements about computer. Which statement is correct about it?

Statement I Computer can store information.

Statement II Computer is similar to typewriter.

Statement III Computer is an electronic machine.

(a) Statement I is correct.

(b) Statement II is correct.

(c) Both statement I and statement III are correct.

(d) Both statement II and statement III are correct.

26. Computer can perform two types of functions: Mathematical and Logical function.

I. + is a logical function.

II. – is used as a mathematical function.

III. > is used as a logical function.

IV. / is a mathematical function.

Which of the above statements is/are correct regarding mathematical functions?

(a) Statement I is correct

(b) Statements II and IV are correct

(c) Statements III and IV are correct

(d) Statements II and III are correct

Darken your choice with HB Pencil

1. (a) (b) (c) (d)	6. (a) (b) (c) (d)	11. (a) (b) (c) (d)	16. (a) (b) (c) (d)	21. (a) (b) (c) (d)	26. (a) (b) (c) (d)
2. (a) (b) (c) (d)	7. (a) (b) (c) (d)	12. (a) (b) (c) (d)	17. (a) (b) (c) (d)	22. (a) (b) (c) (d)	
3. (a) (b) (c) (d)	8. (a) (b) (c) (d)	13. (a) (b) (c) (d)	18. (a) (b) (c) (d)	23. (a) (b) (c) (d)	
4. (a) (b) (c) (d)	9. (a) (b) (c) (d)	14. (a) (b) (c) (d)	19. (a) (b) (c) (d)	24. (a) (b) (c) (d)	
5. (a) (b) (c) (d)	10. (a) (b) (c) (d)	15. (a) (b) (c) (d)	20. (a) (b) (c) (d)	25. (a) (b) (c) (d)	

Main Parts of a Computer

1. Which of the following is used to put your pictures into a computer?

(a) 

(b) 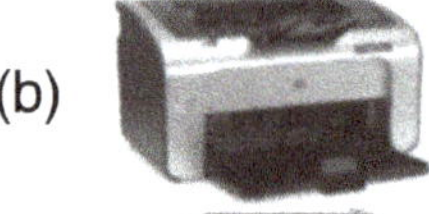

(c) 

(d) 

2. Which of the following is the main part of a computer?

(a) UPS
(b) Microphones
(c) Mouse
(d) CPU

3. This device helps in the .... step of working on an information by a computer.

(a) input
(b) storage
(c) process
(d) output

4. This device helps in the .... step of working on an information by a computer.

(a) input   (b) storage
(c) process   (d) output

5. What type of software is this?

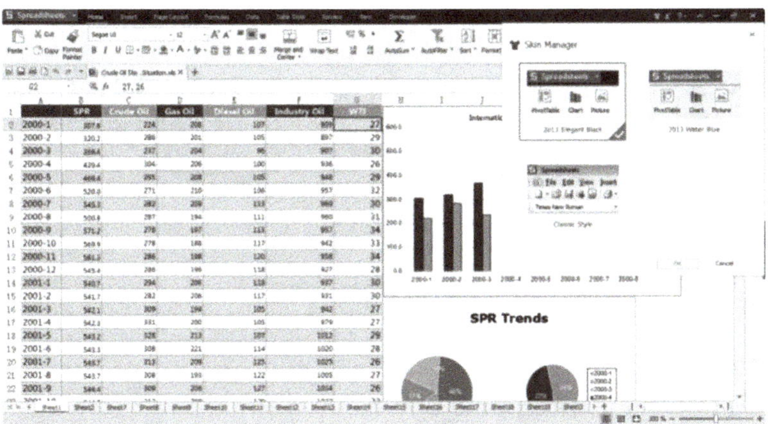

(a) Word processing software   (b) Spreadsheet software
(c) Communication software   (d) Painting software

6. The process of pressing a mouse button for two times is
   (a) double click   (b) single click
   (c) two tImes click   (d) second click

7. Information in memory of a digital computer is stored in
   (a) binary digit (0 and 1)   (b) alphabets (A-Z)
   (c) number (0-9)   (d) None of these

8. Which of the following is both an input and output device?
   (a) Touchscreen   (b) LCD Projector Panel
   (c) Audio Cards   (d) Modem

9. A device that allows the user to see the information generated by computer is called an

(a) input device   (b) storage device

(c) output device   (d) None of these

10. The device that allows to print the output seen in the monitor on paper is

(a) monitor   (b) printer

(c) scanner   (d) All of these

11. Which device will display the pictures and words on a computer?

(a)    (b) 

(c)    (d) 

12. Which of the following statements is/are true?

(a) Calculations are performed in CPU.

(b) CPU controls all the functions of a computer.

(c) CPU is the brain of a computer.

(d) All of the above

13. Which device is used for entering data into a computer?

(a)    (b) 

(c)    (d) 

14. The device shown in the picture is used to

(a) record a voice   (b) listen to sounds
(c) play games   (d) type documents

15. Which part of the computer is missing in the given picture?

(a) Keyboard   (b) Mouse
(c) CPU   (d) Monitor

16. Which of the following is used to connect the different parts of a computer?

(a) Thread   (b) Data cable
(c) Copper wire   (d) Steel wire

17. Which of the following is associated with point, hold and release?

(a) Keyboard   (b) Mouse
(c) Monitor   (d) All of these

18. Through which of the following can a computer think?

(a) Monitor   (b) CPU
(c) Keyboard   (d) Speakers

19. Where does a computer store the information?

    (a) Memory unit   (b) Control unit

    (c) Input unit   (d) Output unit

20. Which of these storage devices can be carried along with the user?

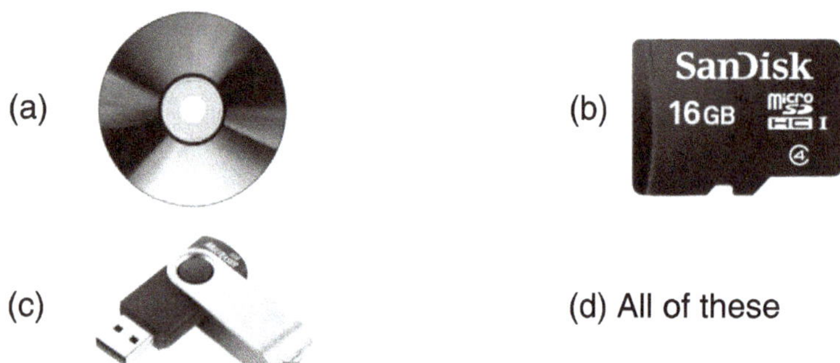

    (a)   (b)

    (c)   (d) All of these

21. Identify the hardware amongst the following.

    (a)   (b) Google

    (c) YouTube   (d) facebook

22. Which of the following is incorrect about the device hidden in scrambled word below?

RPNIRTE

    (a) It helps in displaying output on paper.

    (b) It gives output in only black and white.

    (c) It is a separate device attached to the CPU.

    (d) Different companies sell this device.

23. Data and programs are temporarily stored in

(a) Memory　　　　　　　　　　　(b) Processor

(c) Storage device　　　　　　　　(d) None of these

24. A computer has many parts. There is one part of the computer similar to the TV screen. Which one of the following parts of the computer looks like a typewriter machine?

(a) 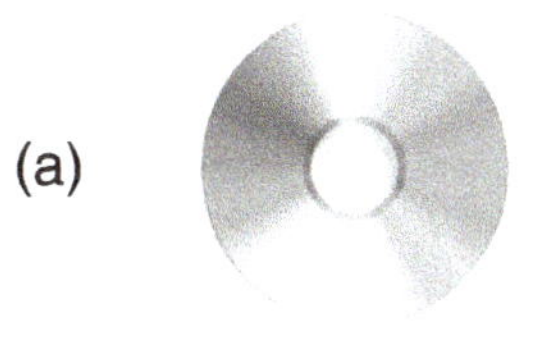　　　　　　　　　(b) 

(c) 　　　　　　　　　(d) 

25. Which of the following options lists all devices used for output from a computer?

(a) LED display monitor, Inkjet printer, Plotter

(b) Flat panel display, Plotter, Barcode scanner

(c) Laser printer, Optical character reader, Plotter

(d) Laser printer, Inkjet printer, Scanner

26. Consider the following statements.

I. Floppy disk has more storage capacity as compared to CD-ROM.

II. CD-ROM has more storage capacity as compared to floppy disk.

Which of the above statements are true?

(a) Only I　　　　　　　　　　　(b) Only II

(c) Both I and II　　　　　　　　(d) Neither I nor II

27. Consider the following statements and unscramble the word.

TOMIRON

I. It displays output on a screen.

II. It looks like a television.

III. We can also hear the music on it.

Which of the above statement(s) is/are incorrect about the scrambled word?

(a) Only I   (b) Only II

(c) Only III   (d) All of these

28. Complete the following words and choose which of the following is incorrectly matched?

	List I	List II
(a)	M _ _ _ TE _	
(b)	_ P _ _ K _ _	
(c)	K _ _ B _ _ R _	
(d)	P _ _ N _ _ R	

29. Which of the following is correctly matched?

(a) Input – Dividing   (b) Processing – Numbers

(c) Output – Result   (d) All of these

Darken your choice with HB Pencil

1.	(a) (b) (c) (d)	**6.**	(a) (b) (c) (d)	**11.**	(a) (b) (c) (d)	**16.**	(a) (b) (c) (d)	**21.**	(a) (b) (c) (d)	**26.**	(a) (b) (c) (d)
2.	(a) (b) (c) (d)	**7.**	(a) (b) (c) (d)	**12.**	(a) (b) (c) (d)	**17.**	(a) (b) (c) (d)	**22.**	(a) (b) (c) (d)	**27.**	(a) (b) (c) (d)
3.	(a) (b) (c) (d)	**8.**	(a) (b) (c) (d)	**13.**	(a) (b) (c) (d)	**18.**	(a) (b) (c) (d)	**23.**	(a) (b) (c) (d)	**28.**	(a) (b) (c) (d)
4.	(a) (b) (c) (d)	**9.**	(a) (b) (c) (d)	**14.**	(a) (b) (c) (d)	**19.**	(a) (b) (c) (d)	**24.**	(a) (b) (c) (d)	**29.**	(a) (b) (c) (d)
5.	(a) (b) (c) (d)	**10.**	(a) (b) (c) (d)	**15.**	(a) (b) (c) (d)	**20.**	(a) (b) (c) (d)	**25.**	(a) (b) (c) (d)		

03

Uses of a Computer

1. At which place, computers are used to store information of patients?
   - (a) School
   - (b) Hospital
   - (c) Airport
   - (d) Library

2. Where can we draw pictures in computers?
   - (a) MS Word
   - (b) MS PowerPoint
   - (c) Paint
   - (d) MS Excel

3. Identify the correct order of steps of how a computer works.
   - (a) Input ---> Process ---> Output
   - (b) Input ---> Output ---> Process
   - (c) Output ---> Process ---> Input
   - (d) Process ---> Output ----> Input

4. This device helps in the .... step of working on an information by a computer.

   - (a) input
   - (b) storage
   - (c) process
   - (d) output

5. Computers are used to book and cancel tickets at/in
   - (a) schools
   - (b) airports
   - (c) home
   - (d) library

6. In which place, computers are used to deposit and withdraw money?
   - (a) Banks
   - (b) Hospital
   - (c) School
   - (d) Airport

7. Computers are used at home for
   (a) making list for shopping   (b) reading stories
   (c) playing games   (d) All of these

8. Computers are used in scientific research for
   (a) entertainment   (b) weather forecasting
   (c) booking tickets   (d) making list of books

9. The computer helps us to buy items for home. This process is popularly known as
   (a) offline shopping   (b) window shopping
   (c) e-shopping   (d) market shopping

10. During Covid lockdown, all schools carried out classes using computers. These type of classes are known as
    (a) computer classes   (b) online classes
    (c) distance classes   (d) covid classes

11. Computer helps to withdraw money from
    (a) PTM   (b) ATN
    (c) APM   (d) ATM

12. Teacher uses computers to make
    (a) movies   (b) bills
    (c) report card   (d) shopping list

13. I am an intelligent machine. I look like human. I am controlled by a computer. Who am I?
    (a) Sports Car   (b) Robot
    (c) Ribbon   (d) Refrigerator

14. Computer helps us to write a letter, book, article or report through an application. What is the name of that application?
    (a) MS Excel   (b) MS PowerPoint
    (c) MS Word   (d) Paint

15. Identify the incorrect statement from the following.

(a) At home, it helps you to do homework, play games and watch movies.

(b) In offices, it helps with typing, printing and sending messages.

(c) In banks, it is used to maintain accounts of customers.

(d) In hospitals, it helps a doctor to put vaccines and injections.

16. Computer works on the basis of input-output processing. The useful information that the computer produces after processing the data is called

(a) output　　　　　　　　　　　　　(b) input

(c) processing　　　　　　　　　　　(d) decision

17. The given symbols '>', '<', '=' are known by which function name?

(a) Mathematical　　　　　　　　　　(b) Arithmetical

(c) Logical　　　　　　　　　　　　　(d) Special

18. At airport, computer gives information about arrival and departure of

(a) ships　　　　　　　　　　　　　　(b) trains

(c) aeroplanes　　　　　　　　　　　(d) taxi

19. Which one of the following features of a computer enables the user to play sound and video on a computer?

(a) Backup feature　　　　　　　　　(b) Disk cleanup utility feature

(c) Multimedia feature　　　　　　　(d) All of these

20. Which of the following pair is incorrectly matched?

(a) I use computer for space research — Doctor

(b) I use computer to teach students — Teacher

(c) I use computer to deposit money of customer — Banker

(d) I use computer to keep a record of stocks at my shop — Shopkeeper

21. Which of the following pairs is correctly matched?

	List I	List II
(a)	The information you write on the form	Input
(b)	Printed tickets	Processing
(c)	Searching the seat as per your requirements	Output
(d)	All of the above	

22. Consider the following statements.

I. Computers are used at airports to book and cancel tickets.

II. Computers are used at railway stations to book and cancel tickets.

Which of the above statements is/are correct?

(a) Only I   (b) Only II

(c) Both I and II   (d) Neither I nor II

23. If Multiply 150 by 250, the result is 37500.
The following are the statements based on the above statement.

I. 500 is input data.

II. It is the information i.e., output.

Which one of the following options is/are true for above statements?

(a) Only I   (b) Only II

(c) Both I and II   (d) Neither I nor II

Darken your choice with HB Pencil

1.	ⓐ ⓑ ⓒ ⓓ	5.	ⓐ ⓑ ⓒ ⓓ	9.	ⓐ ⓑ ⓒ ⓓ	13.	ⓐ ⓑ ⓒ ⓓ	17.	ⓐ ⓑ ⓒ ⓓ	21.	ⓐ ⓑ ⓒ ⓓ
2.	ⓐ ⓑ ⓒ ⓓ	6.	ⓐ ⓑ ⓒ ⓓ	10.	ⓐ ⓑ ⓒ ⓓ	14.	ⓐ ⓑ ⓒ ⓓ	18.	ⓐ ⓑ ⓒ ⓓ	22.	ⓐ ⓑ ⓒ ⓓ
3.	ⓐ ⓑ ⓒ ⓓ	7.	ⓐ ⓑ ⓒ ⓓ	11.	ⓐ ⓑ ⓒ ⓓ	15.	ⓐ ⓑ ⓒ ⓓ	19.	ⓐ ⓑ ⓒ ⓓ	23.	ⓐ ⓑ ⓒ ⓓ
4.	ⓐ ⓑ ⓒ ⓓ	8.	ⓐ ⓑ ⓒ ⓓ	12.	ⓐ ⓑ ⓒ ⓓ	16.	ⓐ ⓑ ⓒ ⓓ	20.	ⓐ ⓑ ⓒ ⓓ		

Introduction to Keys and Keyboard

1. The function keys are from .... to ....
   (a) F1, F2
   (b) F2, F5
   (c) F1, F10
   (d) F1, F12

2. Function keys are located at the.............. of the keyboard.
   (a) above
   (b) below
   (c) top
   (d) mid

3. Which key is used to open the start menu?
   (a) Alt
   (b)
   (c) ⇧Shift
   (d)

4. How many alphabet keys are there on the keyboard?
   (a) 40
   (b) 20
   (c) 26
   (d) 30

5. What is the function of Alt+F4 key?
   (a) To open a new document
   (b) To close window
   (c) To open window
   (d) To shut down the computer

6. The numeric keyboard works only when you press the ....key and keep it ON.
   (a) Caps lock   (b) Num Lock
   (c) Insert   (d) Home

7. .... invented computer keyboard.
   (a) Bill Gates   (b) Tim Cook
   (c) Christopher Sholes   (d) Jeff Bezos

8. Which keys are used to type your name or a complete sentence?
   (a) Alphabet keys   (b) Number keys
   (c) Enter keys   (d) Arrow keys

9. If I have to type I LOVE COMPUTER, which key will I use along with the alphabet keys?
   (a) Number key   (b) Caps Lock key
   (c) Space bar key   (d) Enter key

10. What are these keys called?

   (a) Symbol keys   (b) Punctuation keys
   (c) Number keys   (d) Sentence keys

11. Which key combination is used to save a file in wordpad?
   (a) Ctrl + C   (b) Ctrl + V

   (c) Ctrl + S   (d) None of these

12. Which key allows us to cancel an operation?
    (a) Shift key   (b) Escape key
    (c) Enter key   (d) Space bar key

13. .... key can be used with other keys for various purposes.

    (a) Enter key   (b) Backspace key
    (c) Tab key   (d) Shift key

14. Choose the correct shortcut for performing the following action: Undo an action.
    (a) CTRL + Z   (b) CTRL + mouse scroll button
    (c) CTRL and +   (d) CTRL and –

15. What is a QWERTY keyboard?
    (a) Ergonomic design standard for a keyboard.
    (b) A common style of keyboard.
    (c) A keyboard designed to be used with only one hand.
    (d) A compact keyboard for personal digital assistance devices.

16. There are .... function keys on the top of the keyboard, marked ....to
    (a) 20, F0, F19   (b) 18, F1, F18
    (c) 12, F1, F12   (d) 4, F1, F4

17. There are different types of keys which cannot work independently. Name the key.
    (a) Delete key   (b) Space bar key
    (c) Alt key   (d) Enter key

18. There are various signs on the keyboard which are used for various purposes. For what purpose * (asterisk) sign is used?
    (a) Addition   (b) Multiplication
    (c) Division   (d) Subtraction

19. On every special key character you have seen symbols. What is '#' symbol called?
    (a) Dollar   (b) Hash
    (c) Ampersand   (d) Tilde

20. If Caps Lock is ON and we need to type small letter 'a', we have to press which key?

(a) Alt + A key combination

(b) Ctrl + A key combination

(c) Shift + A key combination

(d) Spacebar + A key combination

21. Which of the following pairs are correctly matched?

	List I (Command)	**List II** (Shortcut)
(a)	Ctrl+P	Print
(b)	Ctrl+C	Copy
(c)	Ctrl+Y	Redo
(d)	All of the above	

22. Identify the correct statement.

(a) We need delete key to move the cursor.

(b) We need to press Ctrl+A to open Task Manager.

(c) We can also call the Enter key as Command key.

(d) Win key is the largest key on the keyboard.

23. Identify the incorrect statement.

(a) A keyboard is an important part of a computer.

(b) Arrow keys allow you to move the cursor in four directions.

(c) The num lock key is pressed to turn the numeric keypad ON and OFF.

(d) The shift key is used to give space between two words.

Darken your choice with HB Pencil

1.	ⓐ ⓑ ⓒ ⓓ	5.	ⓐ ⓑ ⓒ ⓓ	9.	ⓐ ⓑ ⓒ ⓓ	13.	ⓐ ⓑ ⓒ ⓓ	17.	ⓐ ⓑ ⓒ ⓓ	21.	ⓐ ⓑ ⓒ ⓓ
2.	ⓐ ⓑ ⓒ ⓓ	6.	ⓐ ⓑ ⓒ ⓓ	10.	ⓐ ⓑ ⓒ ⓓ	14.	ⓐ ⓑ ⓒ ⓓ	18.	ⓐ ⓑ ⓒ ⓓ	22.	ⓐ ⓑ ⓒ ⓓ
3.	ⓐ ⓑ ⓒ ⓓ	7.	ⓐ ⓑ ⓒ ⓓ	11.	ⓐ ⓑ ⓒ ⓓ	15.	ⓐ ⓑ ⓒ ⓓ	19.	ⓐ ⓑ ⓒ ⓓ	23.	ⓐ ⓑ ⓒ ⓓ
4.	ⓐ ⓑ ⓒ ⓓ	8.	ⓐ ⓑ ⓒ ⓓ	12.	ⓐ ⓑ ⓒ ⓓ	16.	ⓐ ⓑ ⓒ ⓓ	20.	ⓐ ⓑ ⓒ ⓓ		

05

Introduction to Computer Mouse

1. What type of mouse is given in the picture?

  (a) USB mouse   (b) Optical mouse

  (c) Mechanical mouse   (d) Electronic mouse

2. Which of the following is the proper way to use a mouse?

  (a) Use the mouse pad   (b) Point the mouse towards the computer

  (c) Place mouse on the keyboard   (d) Both (a) and (b)

3. What do you do when you press the left mouse button?

  (a) Double click   (b) Left click

  (c) Right click   (d) Both (a) and (b)

4. Which mouse action opens a program?

  (a) Click   (b) Right click

  (c) Double click   (d) Triple click

5. How do you right click on a mouse?

  (a) Press and release right mouse button.

  (b) Press and holding left mouse button.

  (c) Press and holding right mouse button.

  (d) Double click the right mouse button.

6. What is the function of button #3?

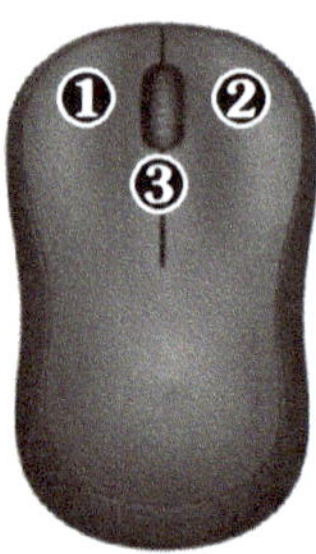

(a) No function

(b) To scroll (move) up or down on a page

(c) To enlarge a page on computer

(d) To move the cursor/arrow

7. Which function is correct for button #1 (left click)?

(a) To write on the computer   (b) To listen to music

(c) To adjust font color   (d) To select a file

8. What is the act of moving a page up and down known as?

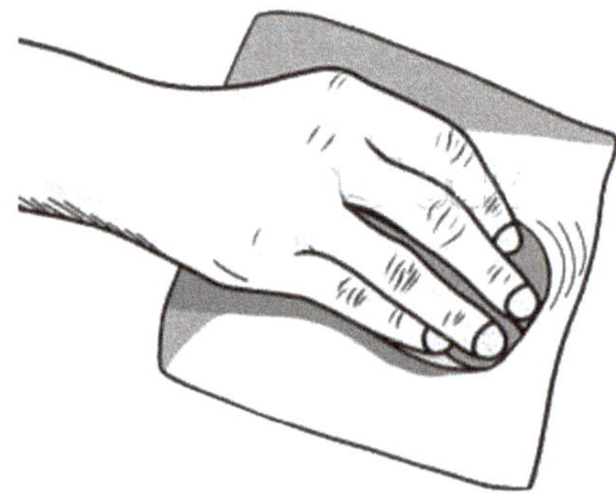

(a) Pointing   (b) Scrolling

(c) Clicking   (d) Checking

9. Nithya gave a right click on the 'My Computer' icon. What did she observe?
   (a) My Computer icon opened.
   (b) The position of My Computer icon was changed.
   (c) The list of commands were displayed on the monitor.
   (d) My Computer icon was deleted.

10. Which of the following is not a function of the mouse?
    (a) Play games   (b) Draw pictures
    (c) Open files   (d) Insert letters

11. Which of the following types of mouse contains a ball on its underside and sensors to find directions of ball movement?
    (a) Mechanical mouse   (b) Opto-mechanical mouse
    (c) Optical mouse   (d) None of these

12. Cordless mouse or wireless mouse connects to the computer through
    (a) Infrared light   (b) Radio wave
    (c) Both (a) and (b)   (d) None of these

13. Optical mouse was developed by .... in 1999. It uses a light beam to detect the movement.
    (a) Apple   (b) Microsoft
    (c) IBM   (d) TATA

14. Changing the place of icons using a mouse is known as
    (a) clicking   (b) double clicking
    (c) dragging   (d) single clicking

15. Name the slant arrow moving on the monitor screen.
    (a) Arrow   (b) Stick
    (c) Mouse pointer   (d) Cursor

16. Which action is same in a mouse and a camera?
    (a) Double-Clicking   (b) Triple-Clicking
    (c) No Clicking   (d) Clicking

17. What do we call a mouse which has no wire?

    (a) Mechanical mouse   (b) Opto-mechanical mouse

    (c) Optical mouse   (d) Wireless mouse

18. Which statement is correct about the mouse from the following options?

    (a) We can use a mouse to draw pictures, select items and play games.

    (b) The movement of a mouse pointer is controlled by a keyboard.

    (c) The pointer always moves towards the right side of the screen.

    (d) Clicking on the left mouse button will show the list of commands.

19. Whereas a computer mouse moves over the table surface, the trackball is

    (a) stationary   (b) difficult to move

    (c) dragged   (d) moves in small steps

20. Which of the following functions is not performed using a mouse?

    (a) Turn on   (b) Hover

    (c) Right-click   (d) Drag and Drop

21. .... is used for detecting mouse motion.

    (a) Optical sensor   (b) Rollers on the bottom of mouse

    (c) Both (a) and (b)   (d) Sensor

22. .... is used to show list of commands or pop up menu on the screen.

    (a) left click   (b) double click

    (c) right click   (d) None of these

23. The .... on the screen is controlled by the mouse.

    (a) text   (b) arrow

    (c) picture   (d) line

Darken your choice with HB Pencil

1. ⓐ ⓑ ⓒ ⓓ	5. ⓐ ⓑ ⓒ ⓓ	9. ⓐ ⓑ ⓒ ⓓ	13. ⓐ ⓑ ⓒ ⓓ	17. ⓐ ⓑ ⓒ ⓓ	21. ⓐ ⓑ ⓒ ⓓ
2. ⓐ ⓑ ⓒ ⓓ	6. ⓐ ⓑ ⓒ ⓓ	10. ⓐ ⓑ ⓒ ⓓ	14. ⓐ ⓑ ⓒ ⓓ	18. ⓐ ⓑ ⓒ ⓓ	22. ⓐ ⓑ ⓒ ⓓ
3. ⓐ ⓑ ⓒ ⓓ	7. ⓐ ⓑ ⓒ ⓓ	11. ⓐ ⓑ ⓒ ⓓ	15. ⓐ ⓑ ⓒ ⓓ	19. ⓐ ⓑ ⓒ ⓓ	23. ⓐ ⓑ ⓒ ⓓ
4. ⓐ ⓑ ⓒ ⓓ	8. ⓐ ⓑ ⓒ ⓓ	12. ⓐ ⓑ ⓒ ⓓ	16. ⓐ ⓑ ⓒ ⓓ	20. ⓐ ⓑ ⓒ ⓓ	

Introduction to MS Paint 2016

1. We can create a mirror image of a stamp using the .... button.
   - (a) cupboard
   - (b) mirror
   - (c) almirah
   - (d) table

2. To access the Fill tool, you click
   - (a) Paint->Fill
   - (b) Fill->Magic
   - (c) Magic->Fill
   - (d) Paint->Magic

3. By using this menu in MS Paint, we can copy and paste selected parts of an image.
   - (a) File
   - (b) Home
   - (c) View
   - (d) Edit

4. Which tool is quite similar to the paint tool?
   - (a) Lines tool
   - (b) Stamp tool
   - (c) Brush tool
   - (d) Select tool

5. What is the function of this tool in MS Paint?

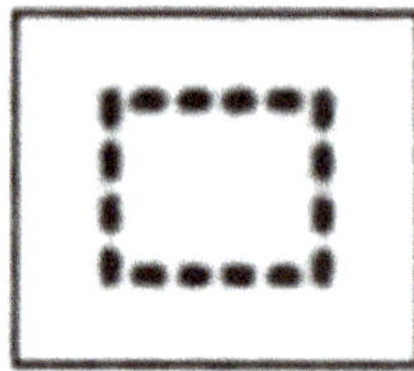

(a) Selects an area of an image in a rectangular shape.

(b) Picks up a color from one area of an image to use with a drawing tool.

(c) Select a free form (irregular sized) object.

(d) Makes a square shape.

6. Which of the following is not a part of paint program?

   (a) shapes   (b) edit

   (c) color   (d) fill

7. Which of the following tools is not available in the Ribbon Bar?

   (a) Clipboard   (b) Image

   (c) Tool   (d) View

8. Which bar is used for moving the page up and down in MS Paint?

   (a) Vertical Scroll Bar   (b) Status Bar

   (c) Horizontal Scroll Bar   (d) Title bar

9. MS Paint application is available in which of the following operating system?

   (a) Linux   (b) Windows

   (c) DOS   (d) MAC OS

10. What cannot be drawn with the use of line tool?

    (a) Circle   (b) Square

    (c) Rectangle   (d) diamond

11. In MS Paint, which bar contains options-select, crop, resize and rotate?

    (a) Image   (b) Tool

    (c) Shape   (d) Color

12. Identify the following tool from its characteristics.

I. It is used for writing anything with a free hand.

II. Press and hold the left mouse button to work.

Codes

(a) Ellipse   (b) Magic

(c) Select   (d) Pencil

13. Which of the following is correctly matched?

	List I	List II
(a)	Text tool	Erases a drawing
(b)	Eraser tool	Used to add text
(c)	Curve tool	Used to draw free form drawing
(d)	Pencil tool	Adds a curved line

Darken your choice with HB Pencil

1. ⓐ ⓑ ⓒ ⓓ	5. ⓐ ⓑ ⓒ ⓓ	9. ⓐ ⓑ ⓒ ⓓ	13. ⓐ ⓑ ⓒ ⓓ
2. ⓐ ⓑ ⓒ ⓓ	6. ⓐ ⓑ ⓒ ⓓ	10. ⓐ ⓑ ⓒ ⓓ	
3. ⓐ ⓑ ⓒ ⓓ	7. ⓐ ⓑ ⓒ ⓓ	11. ⓐ ⓑ ⓒ ⓓ	
4. ⓐ ⓑ ⓒ ⓓ	8. ⓐ ⓑ ⓒ ⓓ	12. ⓐ ⓑ ⓒ ⓓ	

07

Latest Developments in the Field of IT

1. What does the E in e-mail stand for?
   - (a) Excellent
   - (b) Error
   - (c) Electronic
   - (d) Electricity

2. Name the small picture that represents a folder, program or other things.
   - (a) Icon
   - (b) Image
   - (c) Graphic
   - (d) Desktop

3. A worldwide network of computers is termed as
   - (a) Internet
   - (b) Network
   - (c) CPU
   - (d) RAM

4. How can you help to protect your computer from viruses or spam?
   - (a) Don't open e-mails from people you don't know.
   - (b) Don't enter online contests.
   - (c) Don't complete online surveys.
   - (d) All of the above

5. Chrome, Firefox, Safari, Explorer are the examples of
   - (a) operating system software
   - (b) hardware
   - (c) browser
   - (d) search engine

6. You need to create a presentation for your Social Studies class. The presentation will include pictures, text and other graphics. What is the best Google application to use?
   - (a) Google Sheets
   - (b) Google Docs
   - (c) Google Drive
   - (d) Google Slides

7. Your English teacher has asked students to write a short story. She has told you it should be double spaced and have margins of 1 inch. What is the best Google application to use for this assignment?

(a) Google Sheets　　　　　　　　(b) Google Docs

(c) Google Slides　　　　　　　　(d) Google Meet

8. Look at the pictures. Name the page orientation A

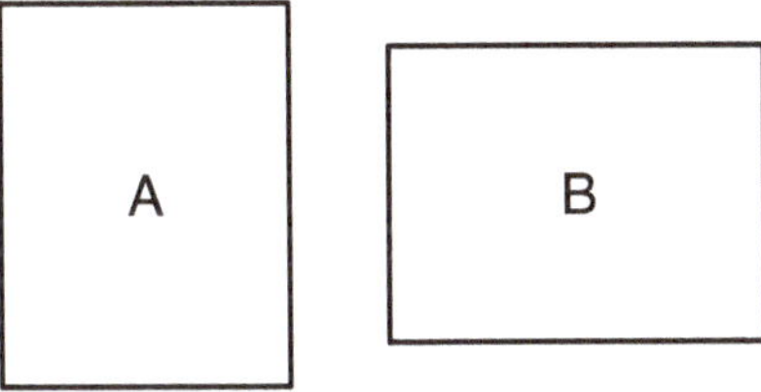

(a) Straight　　　　　　　　(b) Portrait

(c) Horizontal　　　　　　　　(d) Landscape

9. What is the name of the Google Drive location where you store the files you create or upload?

(a) Your Drive　　　　　　　　(b) BC21 Work

(c) My Drive　　　　　　　　(d) BC21 Folder

10. What is the main purpose of Google Maps?

(a) To discover the world.

(b) To find locations in specific places and directions to get there.

(c) To use street view to see places.

(d) To learn about map reading.

11. Which three apps are a good substitute for Microsoft applications?

(a) Drawings, Images and Photos

(b) Word, Excel and PowerPoint

(c) Docs, Sheets and Slides

(d) Gmail, Calendar and Drive

12. The nine squares in the upper right hand corner of your email are an icon for which program?

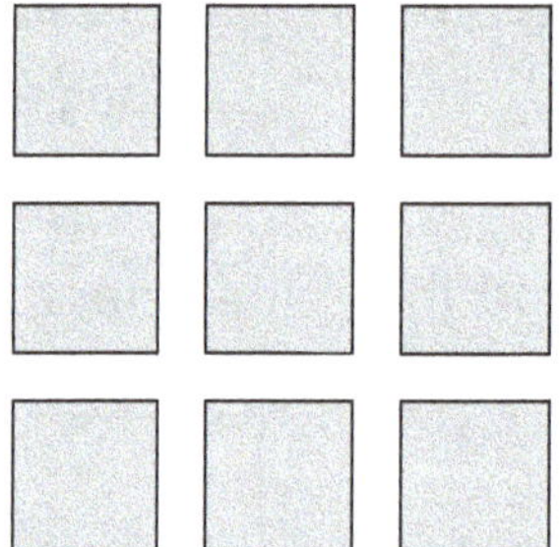

(a) Google Drive   (b) Google Contacts
(c) Google Sheets   (d) Google Apps

13. Which browser is used for Google Classroom?

(a) Safari   (b) Chrome
(c) Firefox   (d) Internet Explorer

14. What does the '+' button do in Google Classroom?

(a) Takes you to Google +   (b) Lets you join a class
(c) Adds a class to your wishlist   (d) Opens a calculator app

15. It is used to collect data and charts.

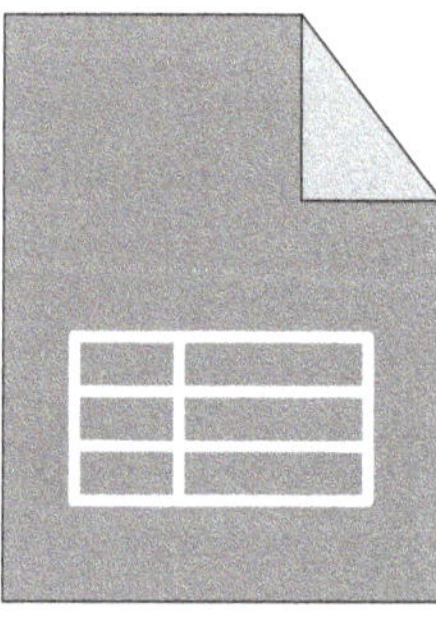

(a) Docs   (b) Slides
(c) Sheets   (d) Forms

16. It is used by teachers and students.

(a) Groups   (b) YouTube
(c) Classroom   (d) Keep

17. What will clicking this icon do for your Google Doc?

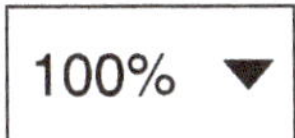

(a) Convert a number to a percentage

(b) Zoom out

(c) Zoom in to actual size of paper

(d) Give you a perfect print

18. How do you share a document with someone?

(a) Put it in a box with a bow on it.

(b) Click the "share" icon and type in their email.

(c) Don't mail them the link.

(d) Tell them to ask nicely.

19. Microsoft Word is equal to Google Docs, so, Microsoft Excel is equal to

(a) Google Docs   (b) Google Classroom
(c) Google Calendar   (d) Google Sheets

20. Which of the following devices can you use to access Google apps?

(a) Smartphone   (b) Tablet
(c) Desktop/laptop   (d) All of these

21. What is the process of moving files from a computer to the internet known as?

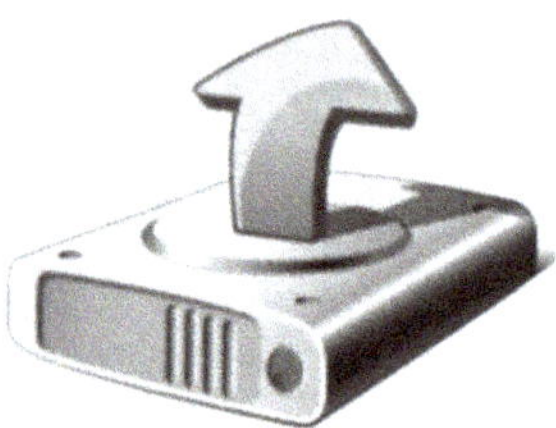

(a) Transfer   (b) Upload
(c) Download   (d) Share

22. What is the process of moving files from internet to your computer known as?

(a) Transfer   (b) Upload
(c) Download   (d) Share

23. With this app, all your photos are backed up safely, organised and labelled automatically, so you can find them quickly and share them however you like. What is the app called as?

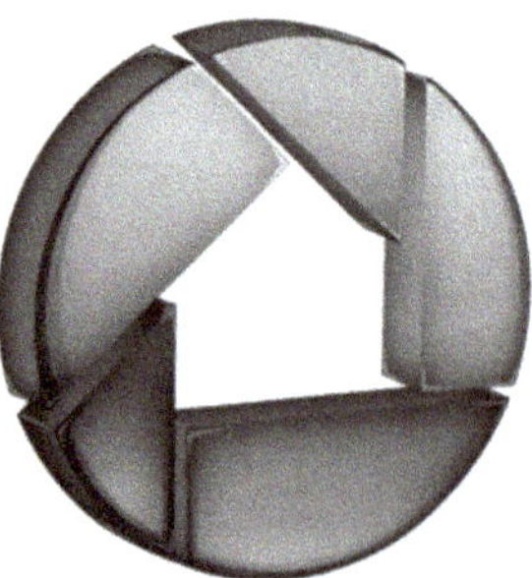

(a) Samsung gallery   (b) Google Doc
(c) Google Sheet   (d) Google Photos

24. Which is the app by Google with which you can explore the 3D view of the world from your computer?

(a) Google Earth   (b) Google Map
(c) Navigator   (d) Drone

25. It is the app through which we can download various other applications, games etc, on Android platform. What is it?

(a) Google Map store   (b) Google distribution store
(c) Google Play store   (d) Google Slide store

26. Which one of the following is the medium for communication between hardware of computer and user?

(a) Application Software   (b) Operating System
(c) Assembler   (d) System Software

27. Which one of the following is not a part of Windows Desktop screen?

(a) Recycle bin   (b) Icons
(c) Taskbar   (d) Paint Brush

Darken your choice with HB Pencil

1.	(a) (b) (c) (d)	6.	(a) (b) (c) (d)	11.	(a) (b) (c) (d)	16.	(a) (b) (c) (d)	21.	(a) (b) (c) (d)	26.	(a) (b) (c) (d)
2.	(a) (b) (c) (d)	7.	(a) (b) (c) (d)	12.	(a) (b) (c) (d)	17.	(a) (b) (c) (d)	22.	(a) (b) (c) (d)	27.	(a) (b) (c) (d)
3.	(a) (b) (c) (d)	8.	(a) (b) (c) (d)	13.	(a) (b) (c) (d)	18.	(a) (b) (c) (d)	23.	(a) (b) (c) (d)		
4.	(a) (b) (c) (d)	9.	(a) (b) (c) (d)	14.	(a) (b) (c) (d)	19.	(a) (b) (c) (d)	24.	(a) (b) (c) (d)		
5.	(a) (b) (c) (d)	10.	(a) (b) (c) (d)	15.	(a) (b) (c) (d)	20.	(a) (b) (c) (d)	25.	(a) (b) (c) (d)		

Practice Sets

1-3

Practice Set 01

Time : 60 Mins.   Max. Marks : 35

General Instructions

1. This question paper contains 35 questions.
2. All questions are compulsory. There is no negative marking.
3. Use HB pencil / Blue ball point pen to mark your choice of answer by darkening the circles on the OMR Sheet.

1. A computer gives output after performing necessary task. Which one of the following parts of a computer executes the logical or arithmetic instructions?

   (a) Monitor (b) CPU

   (c) Mouse (d) Keyboard

2. Which one of the following connects external device with the CPU?

   (a) Steel wire (b) Nuts and bolts

   (c) Data cables (d) All of these

3. Computer is very useful for us and has many important characteristics. Which one of the following is the important characteristic of a computer?

   (a) It has self-intelligence.

   (b) It shares happiness.

   (c) It provides accuracy.

   (d) You can share your sadness.

4. Which of the following statements is/are correct about an app?

   (a) It is an application software.

   (b) It is designed to help the user to perform specific tasks.

   (c) It is available freely or at a nominal price.

   (d) All of the above

5. The given image is of a wearable device called as

(a) Smart watch   (b) Operating watch
(c) Analog watch   (d) Time watch

6. iPad, Google Nexus and Microsoft Surface are examples of …… computers.

(a) Laptop   (b) Tablet
(c) Desktop   (d) Super

7. Which of the following is/are gaming device(s)?

(a) PlayStation   (b) Xbox
(c) Wii   (d) All of these

8. The given device can be read by

(a) Smartphones   (b) Tablets
(c) Calculators   (d) Both (a) and (b)

9. Identify the following mouse action.

   I. It means pressing and releasing the mouse buttons.
   II. It is done after pointing at an item on the screen.

(a) Clicking   (b) Nicking
(c) Ticking   (d) All of these

10. On a computer monitor, a small arrow that moves as you move the mouse is known as
    (a) pointer
    (b) icon
    (c) screen
    (d) None of these

11. The mouse which has a rubber or a metal ball under it is
    (a) Mechanical mouse
    (b) Optical mouse
    (c) 3D mouse
    (d) Tactile mouse

12. If we want to select more than one icon on computer, it can be done with the help of .... the mouse.

    (a) Clicking and dragging
    (b) Double clicking
    (c) Triple clicking
    (d) Quad clicking

13. What does CPU stand for?
    (a) Compressed Program Unit
    (b) Central Processing Unit
    (c) Closed Processing Unit
    (d) Computer Program Unit

14. A monitor is also known as the
    (a) keyboard
    (b) TV
    (c) Visual Display Unit
    (d) book

15. Which of the following is/are multimedia device(s)?
    (a)
    (b)
    (c)
    (d) Both (a) and (b)

16. Identify the devices that store information permanently.

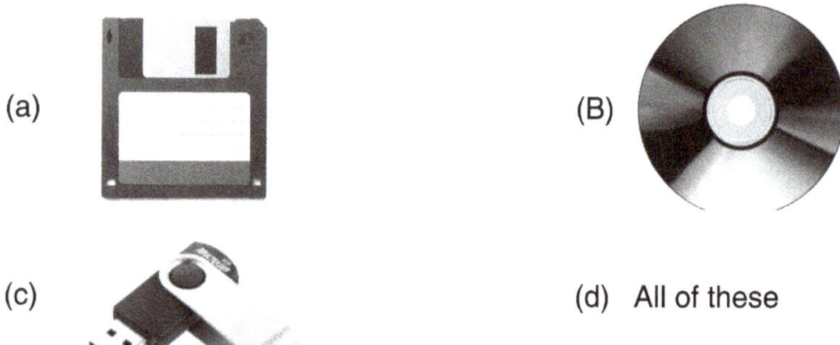

(a)   (B)

(c)   (d) All of these

17. Which of the following device records videos and takes the photographs?

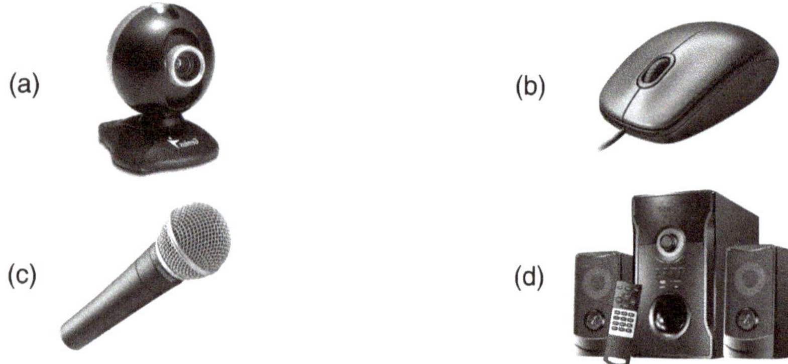

(a)   (b)

(c)   (d)

18. Which of the following is the function of 'Edit Colors' option in MS Paint?
   (a) To change colors of paint ribbon.
   (b) To change a colored picture into black and white.
   (c) To add new colors to color palette.
   (d) All of the above

19. The most commonly used free hand drawing tool is the .... tool.
   (a) paint   (b) color   (c) pencil   (d) eraser

20. .... tool is used to fill color in an object.
   (a) Fill color   (b) Dip color
   (c) Fade color   (d) Bright color

21. Which of the following is used to display margin settings in the MS Word?
   (a) Title Bar   (b) File Tab
   (c) Ruler   (d) Ribbon

22. Name the tool that is used to draw straight patterns.
    (a) Line tool   (b) Pencil tool
    (c) Save tool   (d) Bricks tool

23. Which key will erase the typed data on the current position of the cursor?
    (a) Delete   (b) ⇧Shift

    (c) Alt   (d) Ctrl

24. Which keys in the keyboard are also known as direction keys?
    (a) Arrow keys   (b) Cursor control keys
    (c) Shift keys   (d) Both (a) and (b)

25. Which of the following keys is used to type the symbol # ?
    (a) ⇧Shift + # 3   (b) Alt + # 3

    (c) Ctrl + # 3   (d) ↑ + # 3

26. What is the purpose of Space the key?
    (a) To insert a blank space.   (b) To move to the next line.
    (c) To execute a command.   (d) To exit from a command.

27. On which key is the (→) symbol found?
    (a) Shift key   (b) Arrow key
    (c) Ctrl key   (d) Enter key

28. What is the collection of information about a particular person or object called?
    (a) File   (b) Record
    (c) Program   (d) Table

29. What is/are the purpose(s) of computers in schools?
    (a) For maintaining fee records.
    (b) For maintaining student records.
    (c) For writing circulars.
    (d) All of the above

30. In films, which of the following are created using computers?

(a) Books   (b) Animations

(c) Tickets   (d) Results

31. Which is used for creating cartoons and animation movies?

(a) 

(b) 

(c) 

(d) 

32. In which organisation, does a computer maintain details of patients?

(a) Banks   (b) Schools

(c) Hospitals   (d) Airports

33. Given below are the parts of a computer and its functions. Match the following lists.

	List I		List II
A.	Monitor	1.	Work like a typewriter
B.	CPU	2.	Resemblance with the mouse
C.	Mouse	3.	Display the commands
D.	Keyboard	4.	Work like a brain

Codes

	A	B	C	D
(a)	4	3	2	1
(b)	1	2	3	4
(c)	3	1	2	4
(d)	3	4	2	1

34. Match the following lists with respect to the number of available keys on the keyboard.

	List I		List II
A.	Enter key	1.	12
B.	Backspace key	2.	2
C.	Function key	3.	1

Codes

	A	B	C			A	B	C
(a)	2	3	1		(b)	2	1	3
(c)	3	1	2		(d)	3	2	1

35. Match the following mouse actions given in List I with their corresponding functions in List II.

	List I		List II
A.	Double click	1.	Selects an item
B.	Right click	2.	Opens a program/file
C.	Single click	3.	Moves an item on the screen
D.	Drag and drop	4.	Shows the list of commands on the screen

Codes

	A	B	C	D			A	B	C	D
(a)	3	1	4	2		(b)	1	4	3	2
(c)	1	2	4	3		(d)	2	4	1	3

Practice Set 02

Time : 60 Mins.   Max. Marks : 35

General Instructions

1. This question paper contains 35 questions.
2. All questions are compulsory. There is no negative marking.
3. Use HB pencil / Blue ball point pen to mark your choice of answer by darkening the circles on the OMR Sheet.

1. Starting the computer is also called ……… the system.
   (a) Booting
   (b) Nooting
   (c) Rooting
   (d) Dooting

2. Which of the following options is not present in the Shutdown button of Start menu?
   (a) Lock
   (b) Log off
   (c) Log In
   (d) Sleep

3. What is the full form of GPS?
   (a) Global Positioning System
   (b) Global Packet System
   (c) Geo Positioning System
   (d) Geometrical Position System

4. Identify the given logo.

   (a) Apple play store
   (b) Google play store
   (c) Windows store
   (d) Android play store

5. …… is an online photo-sharing, video sharing and social networking service.

   (a) 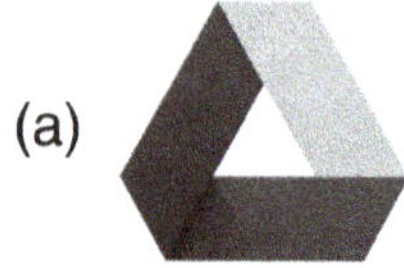
   (b) 
   (c) 
   (d) 

6. Identify the name of the built-in app with respect to Windows 8.1.

   (a) World   (b) People
   (c) Chat   (d) Mail

7. ……… is the developer of Android mobile operating system.
   (a) Google   (b) Yahoo
   (c) Apple Inc   (d) Samsung

8. Which of the following mouse actions is correct if you want  icon to be highlighted on the screen?
   (a) Double click on this icon
   (b) Left click on this icon
   (c) Triple click on this icon
   (d) Drop this icon

9. What should you do when the mouse pointer goes off the screen?
   (a) Click the mouse   (b) Press the space bar
   (c) Wiggle the mouse   (d) Tap the mouse gently

10. Select the correct match.

   (a)  - Trackball   (b) 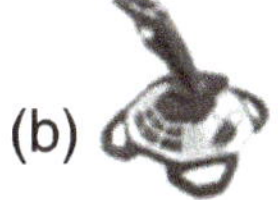 - Optical mouse

   (c)  - Joystick   (d) 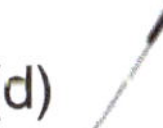 - Pen mouse

11. When we click the left mouse button and drag the mouse without releasing the button, it is known as
   (a) Deselecting   (b) Click and Drag
   (c) Drop and Release   (d) None of these

12. Identify the mouse from the following.

(a) 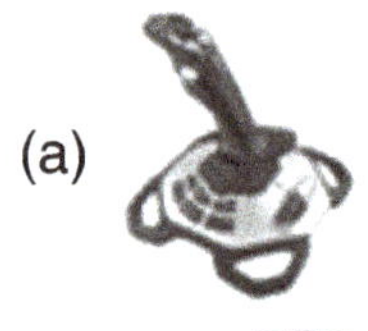   (b) 

(c)    (d) 

13. Which of the following is an input device?

(a) 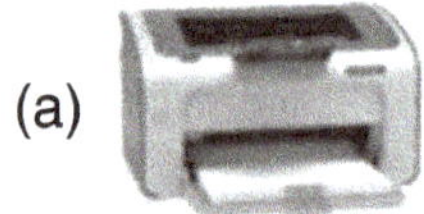   (b) 

(c)    (d) 

14. Which one of these devices is specially used to play games?

(a)    (b) 

(c)    (d) 

15. iPad Mini is a smaller and lighter version of the
(a) Apple iPad Tablet   (b) Samsung Tablet
(c) Microsoft Tablet   (d) Google Tablet

16. Which of the following is not a part of a computer?

(a)    (b) 

(c)    (d) 

17. Which of the following steps will be chosen in MS Paint to get the size of Drawing Area?

(a) File → Properties   (b) Canvas → Resize

(c) File → Page Setup   (d) Image → Resize

18. Which is the Paint tool?

(a) 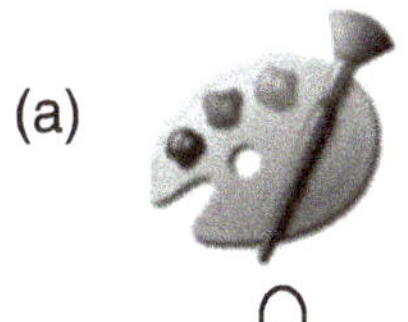   (b) 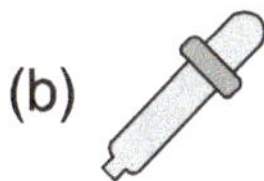

(c)    (d) All of these

19. What is the function of an Enter key?

(a) To move to the next line.   (b) To give space.

(c) To type small and capital letters.   (d) To type numbers.

20. When you press the Ctrl + Alt + Delete keys, which of the following is/are displayed?

(a) 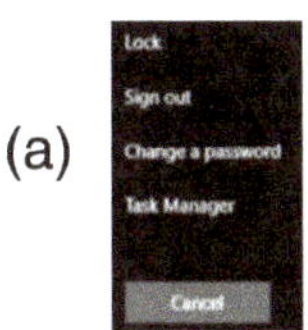   (b) 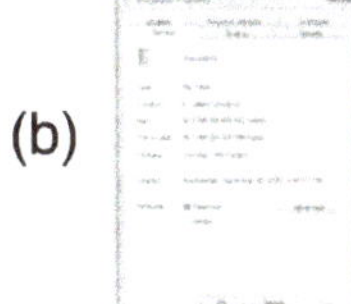

(c) 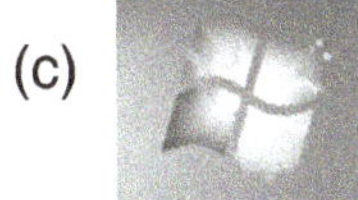   (d) All of these

21. Choose which of the following is a gaming device.

(a) Wii   (b) X box   (c) Play Station   (d) All of these

22. What is the part labelled (X) of the keyboard called?

(a) Cursor control keys   (b) Arrow keys

(c) Numeric keypad   (d) Alphabet keys

23. On which key is ⇤ symbol observed?

   (a) Ctrl key   (b) Alt key

   (c) Tab key   (d) Shift key

24. Which is the Eraser tool?

   (a)   (b)

   (c)   (d)

25. Which key will erase information from the computer's memory and characters on the screen?

   (a) Edit   (b) Delete key

   (c) Dummy out   (d) Trust key

26. Which of the following statements is/are true?

   (a) Computers are used for diagnosing diseases.

   (b) Computers can perform operations.

   (c) Computers are useful for preparing medical reports of patients.

   (d) All of the above

27. Computers are used for sending messages through

   (a) E-mail   (b) phone

   (c) printer   (d) keyboard

28. Which of the following stores a lot of information?

   (a)   (b)

   (c)   (d)

29. Which of the following things can be done on smartphone?

    (a) Listening to music   (b) Solving sums

    (c) Playing games   (d) All of these

30. Which of the following is/are designed using computers?

    (a) Clothes   (b) Aeroplanes

    (c) Cars   (d) All of these

31. Which of the following shows the correct order of Input-Output cycle?

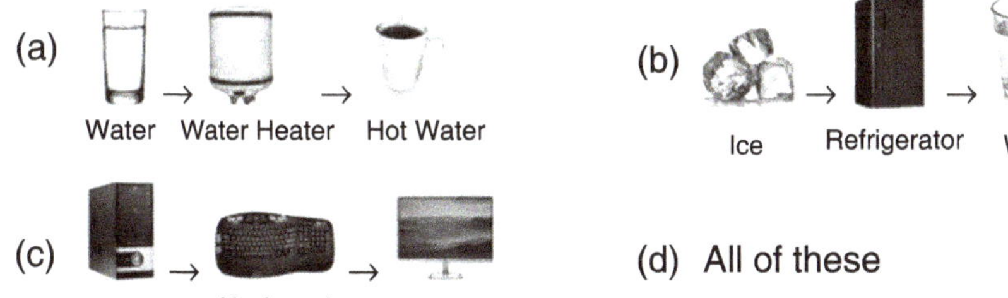

32. Which is the Magic tool?

33. The bar given here, shows the applications that are currently being used by you. It even displays date and time. It is called ……… .

    (a) Taskbar   (b) Start Bar

    (c) Window Bar   (d) Date and time bar

34. Which of the following statements hold(s) true regarding double click?

   I. To release the left mouse button after pressing it twice quickly is called double click.

   II. It opens the selected item.

   Codes

   (a) Only I   (b) Only II

   (c) Both I and II   (d) Neither I nor II

35. Which of the following keys is incorrectly matched?

	Lists I	Lists II
(a)	Alphabet key	C
(b)	Function key	F1
(c)	Number key	! 1
(d)	Windows key	←

Darken your choice with HB Pencil

1. ⓐ ⓑ ⓒ ⓓ	7. ⓐ ⓑ ⓒ ⓓ	13. ⓐ ⓑ ⓒ ⓓ	19. ⓐ ⓑ ⓒ ⓓ	25. ⓐ ⓑ ⓒ ⓓ	31. ⓐ ⓑ ⓒ ⓓ
2. ⓐ ⓑ ⓒ ⓓ	8. ⓐ ⓑ ⓒ ⓓ	14. ⓐ ⓑ ⓒ ⓓ	20. ⓐ ⓑ ⓒ ⓓ	26. ⓐ ⓑ ⓒ ⓓ	32. ⓐ ⓑ ⓒ ⓓ
3. ⓐ ⓑ ⓒ ⓓ	9. ⓐ ⓑ ⓒ ⓓ	15. ⓐ ⓑ ⓒ ⓓ	21. ⓐ ⓑ ⓒ ⓓ	27. ⓐ ⓑ ⓒ ⓓ	33. ⓐ ⓑ ⓒ ⓓ
4. ⓐ ⓑ ⓒ ⓓ	10. ⓐ ⓑ ⓒ ⓓ	16. ⓐ ⓑ ⓒ ⓓ	22. ⓐ ⓑ ⓒ ⓓ	28. ⓐ ⓑ ⓒ ⓓ	34. ⓐ ⓑ ⓒ ⓓ
5. ⓐ ⓑ ⓒ ⓓ	11. ⓐ ⓑ ⓒ ⓓ	17. ⓐ ⓑ ⓒ ⓓ	23. ⓐ ⓑ ⓒ ⓓ	29. ⓐ ⓑ ⓒ ⓓ	35. ⓐ ⓑ ⓒ ⓓ
6. ⓐ ⓑ ⓒ ⓓ	12. ⓐ ⓑ ⓒ ⓓ	18. ⓐ ⓑ ⓒ ⓓ	24. ⓐ ⓑ ⓒ ⓓ	30. ⓐ ⓑ ⓒ ⓓ	

Practice Set 03

Time : 60 Mins.   Max. Marks : 35

General Instructions
1. This question paper contains 35 questions.
2. All questions are compulsory. There is no negative marking.
3. Use HB pencil / Blue ball point pen to mark your choice of answer by darkening the circles on the OMR Sheet.

1. The given device is placed on

(a) 

(b) 

(c) 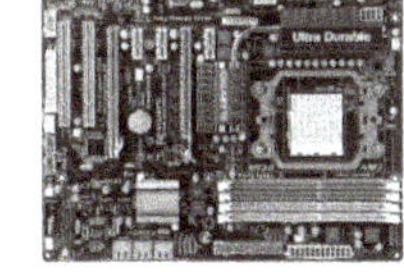

(d) All of these

2. Pen-drive is a ……… device.
   (a) fixed   (b) driver
   (c) storage   (d) input

3. Which of the following words when unscrambled can be used to complete the characteristic of the computer given below?
   Computer is a ……… machine.
   (a) LOWS   (b) BUDM
   (c) MARTS   (d) DIGIR

4. Rini wants to type the symbol %. Which key should she press along with 5?

(a) ⇧Shift   (b) ←

(c) Num Lock   (d) Delete

5. Unscramble the jumbled word given below and select the correct statement about it.

                              EATBLT

(a) It cannot be carried from one place to another.

(b) It can only be used by scientists.

(c) It works with the help of battery, that can be charged with electricity.

(d) All of the above

6. Which of the following is the latest version of Windows operating system as of February, 2016?

(a) Windows Vista   (b) Windows 10

(c) Windows Bigger   (d) Windows 14

7. Which of the following statement(s) is/are the correct difference between Windows 7 and Windows 8.1?

(a) Unlike Windows 8.1, Windows 7 has a start screen.

(b) Windows 7 works with a mouse and keyboard whereas Windows 8.1 can not work with mouse and keyboard.

(c) Unlike Windows 7, Windows 8.1 is built for touch PCs and tablets and has Start screen.

(d) All of the above

8. Which of the following things can be done on smartphones?

(a) Playing games   (b) Listening music

(c) Solving sums   (d) All of these

9. Which of the following can be easily carried from one place to another and also has touchscreen?

(a) Laptop   (b) Smartphone

(c) Desktop Computer   (d) All of these

10. Which of the following is a voice assistant by Microsoft windows ?

(a) Siri   (b) Cortana

(c) Google assistant   (d) Smartphone

11. In the given image, list of properties is displayed for the selected item. Which of the following mouse actions will enable this?

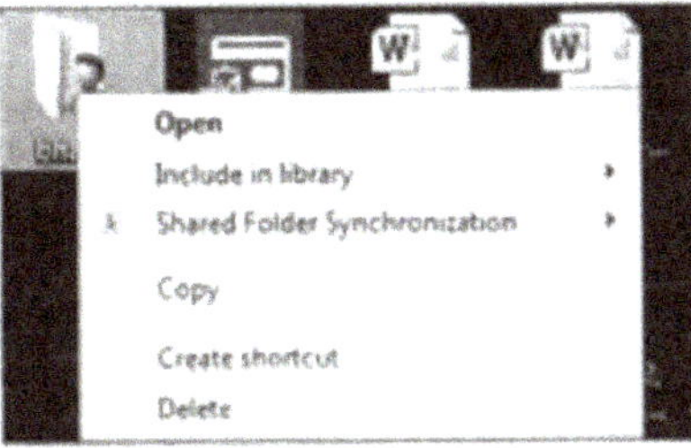

(a) Left Click   (b) Double Click

(c) Right Click   (d) Drag and Drop

12. Rearrange the given steps in correct order to perform drag and drop on computer screen.

I. Click on it to select.

II. Move and bring the mouse pointer to the item which you want to move.

III. Pull the item to the desired location (Drag) and release the button (Drop).

IV. Press and hold the left button of the mouse.

Codes

(a) II → I → IV → III   (b) I → II → III → IV

(c) II → IV → I → III   (d) IV → I → II → III

13. Which of the following mouse actions when performed on 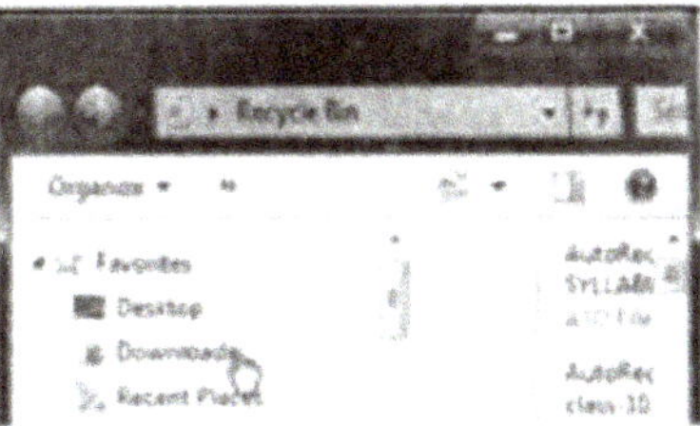 icon will display the given window?

(a) Left Click   (b) Right Click

(c) Double Click   (d) Drag and Drop

14. Which of the following mouse actions would you choose to put the Teddy bear inside the home?

Teddy Bear   Home

(a) Double-click on the Teddy bear   (b) Drag and drop the Teddy bear
(c) Right-click on the Teddy bear   (d) Single-click on the Teddy bear

15. In the context of a mouse, which of the following statements is/are correct?

(a) Left click is when you quickly press and release the left mouse button twice.

(b) We use the left click to select icons and buttons.

(c) The wireless mouse is always connected to the computer monitor.

(d) All of the above

16. Result displayed on the screen of monitor is called

(a) a hard copy   (b) a xerox copy
(c) a paper copy   (d) a soft copy

17. Consider the following statements about given pictures.

Recycle Bin   Network   My Computer

I. They are small pictures, that appear on the display screen (or desktop).

II. They are known as icons. An icon helps us to choose an item on computer screen.

Which of the above statements are true regarding the given pictures?

(a) Only I   (b) Only II
(c) Both I and II   (d) Neither I nor II

18. Which of the following is a storage device?

(a)    (b) 

(c)    (d) Both (a) and (b)

19. ……… is used to connect the different parts of a computer.
   (a) Thread   (b) Data cable
   (c) Copper wire   (d) Steel wire

20. Which device is used for scanning pictures to a computer?

(a)    (b) 

(c)    (d) 

21. What is the function of the following tool?

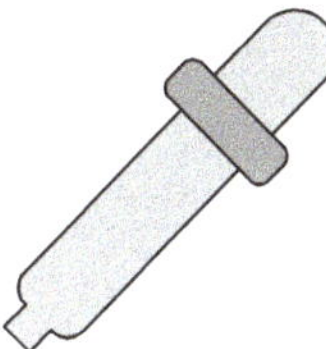

   (a) To delete picture   (b) To pick color from picture
   (c) To select drawing area   (d) To fill picturc with color

22. Which of the following is the use of computer at home?
   (a) To plan monthly budgets
   (b) To keep accounts of employee
   (c) To prepare reports
   (d) All of the above

23. The given information is about which part of the computer?
It controls all the functions of the computer.
(a) Monitor   (b) Speaker
(c) Keyboard   (d) CPU

24. What is the function of the app given below?

(a) Ride a car   (b) Online class
(c) Cook food   (d) Play game

25. In which of the following area of Paint window, you can draw a triangle?
(a) Tools area   (b) Drawing area
(c) File area   (d) Crawling area

26. Which of following keys help you to move the cursor in different directions?

(a) 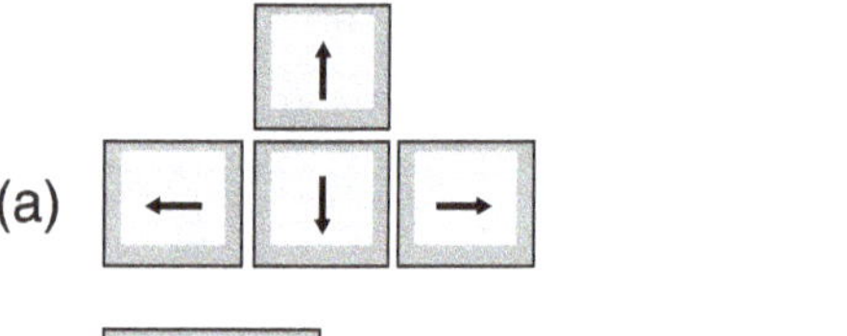   (b) ⇧Shift

(c) Enter   (d) Caps Lock

27. Which button of keyboard makes characters either upper or lower case
and numbers to symbols?
(a) Shift key   (b) Ctrl key
(c) Enter key   (d) Delete key

28. What is meant by keys of the keyboard?
(a) Buttons placed on the keyboard.
(b) Wires placed on the keyboard.
(c) Both (a) and (b)
(d) Neither (a) nor (b)

29. Identify the devices X and Y with the help of given information and choose the correct option for them.

Device X-It is not portable   Device Y-It comes with a touchpad

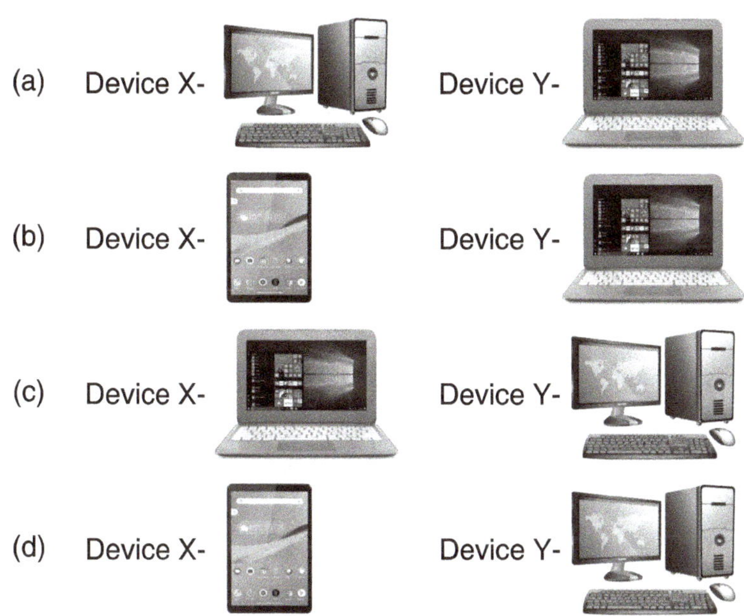

(a) Device X-   Device Y-

(b) Device X-   Device Y-

(c) Device X-   Device Y-

(d) Device X-   Device Y-

30. Which key takes the cursor to the right?

(a) 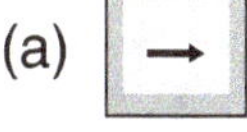   (b) 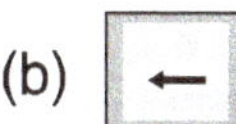

(c) 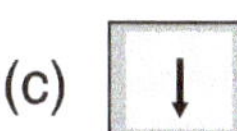   (d) 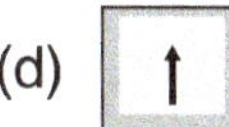

31. Which organisation uses computers for printing and designing newspapers?

(a) Hospitals   (b) Designing

(c) Colleges   (d) Publishing

32. By which of the following you can select icons using a mouse?

(a) Right Click

(b) Left Click

(c) By moving cursor over icon

(d) All of the above

33. Which device is used to print Railway/Bus tickets?

(a) 

(b) 

(c) 

(d) 

34. Which of the following click of mouse displays a list of properties of the selected item?

(a) Right Click   (b) Drop Click
(c) Drag Click   (d) Double Click

35. How is a computer used in space research?

(a) Launching satellites   (b) Printing magazines
(c) Designing cars   (d) Sending messages

Darken your choice with HB Pencil

1.	ⓐ ⓑ ⓒ ⓓ	7.	ⓐ ⓑ ⓒ ⓓ	13.	ⓐ ⓑ ⓒ ⓓ	19.	ⓐ ⓑ ⓒ ⓓ	25.	ⓐ ⓑ ⓒ ⓓ	31.	ⓐ ⓑ ⓒ ⓓ
2.	ⓐ ⓑ ⓒ ⓓ	8.	ⓐ ⓑ ⓒ ⓓ	14.	ⓐ ⓑ ⓒ ⓓ	20.	ⓐ ⓑ ⓒ ⓓ	26.	ⓐ ⓑ ⓒ ⓓ	32.	ⓐ ⓑ ⓒ ⓓ
3.	ⓐ ⓑ ⓒ ⓓ	9.	ⓐ ⓑ ⓒ ⓓ	15.	ⓐ ⓑ ⓒ ⓓ	21.	ⓐ ⓑ ⓒ ⓓ	27.	ⓐ ⓑ ⓒ ⓓ	33.	ⓐ ⓑ ⓒ ⓓ
4.	ⓐ ⓑ ⓒ ⓓ	10.	ⓐ ⓑ ⓒ ⓓ	16.	ⓐ ⓑ ⓒ ⓓ	22.	ⓐ ⓑ ⓒ ⓓ	28.	ⓐ ⓑ ⓒ ⓓ	34.	ⓐ ⓑ ⓒ ⓓ
5.	ⓐ ⓑ ⓒ ⓓ	11.	ⓐ ⓑ ⓒ ⓓ	17.	ⓐ ⓑ ⓒ ⓓ	23.	ⓐ ⓑ ⓒ ⓓ	29.	ⓐ ⓑ ⓒ ⓓ	35.	ⓐ ⓑ ⓒ ⓓ
6.	ⓐ ⓑ ⓒ ⓓ	12.	ⓐ ⓑ ⓒ ⓓ	18.	ⓐ ⓑ ⓒ ⓓ	24.	ⓐ ⓑ ⓒ ⓓ	30.	ⓐ ⓑ ⓒ ⓓ		

Answer Sheet

Chapter 1

1. (c)	2. (a)	3. (b)	4. (b)	5. (b)	6. (b)	7. (c)	8. (c)	9. (c)	10. (c)
11. (d)	12. (d)	13. (c)	14. (d)	15. (a)	16. (c)	17. (b)	18. (d)	19. (c)	20. (c)
21. (c)	22. (a)	23. (c)	24. (c)	25. (c)	26. (b)				

Chapter 2

1. (c)	2. (d)	3. (c)	4. (d)	5. (b)	6. (a)	7. (a)	8. (a)	9. (c)	10. (b)
11. (a)	12. (d)	13. (b)	14. (a)	15. (b)	16. (b)	17. (b)	18. (b)	19. (a)	20. (d)
21. (a)	22. (b)	23. (a)	24. (c)	25. (c)	26. (b)	27. (c)	28. (d)	29. (c)	

Chapter 3

1. (b)	2. (c)	3. (a)	4. (a)	5. (b)	6. (a)	7. (d)	8. (b)	9. (c)	10. (b)
11. (d)	12. (c)	13. (b)	14. (c)	15. (d)	16. (a)	17. (c)	18. (c)	19. (c)	20. (a)
21. (a)	22. (c)	23. (b)							

Chapter 4

1. (d)	2. (c)	3. (d)	4. (c)	5. (b)	6. (b)	7. (c)	8. (a)	9. (b)	10. (b)
11. (c)	12. (b)	13. (d)	14. (a)	15. (b)	16. (c)	17. (c)	18. (b)	19. (b)	20. (c)
21. (d)	22. (c)	23. (d)							

Chapter 5

1. (b)	2. (d)	3. (b)	4. (c)	5. (a)	6. (b)	7. (d)	8. (b)	9. (c)	10. (d)
11. (a)	12. (c)	13. (b)	14. (c)	15. (c)	16. (d)	17. (d)	18. (a)	19. (a)	20. (a)
21. (c)	22. (c)	23. (b)							

Chapter 6

1. (b)	2. (a)	3. (b)	4. (c)	5. (a)	6. (b)	7. (d)	8. (a)	9. (b)	10. (a)
11. (a)	12. (d)	13. (d)							

Chapter 7

1. (c)	2. (a)	3. (a)	4. (d)	5. (c)	6. (d)	7. (b)	8. (b)	9. (c)	10. (b)
11. (c)	12. (b)	13. (b)	14. (b)	15. (c)	16. (c)	17. (c)	18. (b)	19. (d)	20. (d)
21. (b)	22. (c)	23. (d)	24. (a)	25. (c)	26. (b)	27. (d)			

Practice Set 1

1. (b)	2. (c)	3. (c)	4. (d)	5. (a)	6. (b)	7. (d)	8. (d)	9. (a)	10. (a)
11. (a)	12. (a)	13. (b)	14. (c)	15. (d)	16. (d)	17. (a)	18. (c)	19. (c)	20. (a)
21. (c)	22. (a)	23. (a)	24. (d)	25. (a)	26. (a)	27. (d)	28. (b)	29. (d)	30. (b)
31. (a)	32. (c)	33. (d)	34. (a)	35. (d)					

Practice Set 2

1. (a)	2. (c)	3. (a)	4. (b)	5. (c)	6. (b)	7. (a)	8. (b)	9. (c)	10. (a)
11. (b)	12. (c)	13. (d)	14. (a)	15. (a)	16. (d)	17. (a)	18. (d)	19. (a)	20. (a)
21. (d)	22. (c)	23. (c)	24. (c)	25. (b)	26. (d)	27. (a)	28. (b)	29. (d)	30. (d)
31. (a)	32. (b)	33. (a)	34. (c)	35. (d)					

Practice Set 3

1. (c)	2. (c)	3. (c)	4. (a)	5. (c)	6. (b)	7. (c)	8. (d)	9. (b)	10. (b)
11. (c)	12. (a)	13. (c)	14. (b)	15. (b)	16. (d)	17. (c)	18. (d)	19. (b)	20. (b)
21. (b)	22. (a)	23. (d)	24. (b)	25. (b)	26. (a)	27. (a)	28. (a)	29. (a)	30. (a)
31. (d)	32. (b)	33. (a)	34. (a)	35. (a)					